Minis

Leadership Teams

Theory and Practice in Effective Collaborative Ministry

Andrew Dawswell

Vicar of Knypersley

GROVE BOOKS LIMITED

RIDLEY HALL RD CAMBRIDGE CB3 9HU

Contents

The Cover Illustration is by Peter Ashton

First Impression March 2003
ISSN 0144-171X
ISBN 1 85174 525 4

Ministry Leadership Teams: Rhetoric and Reality

1

One of the most radical developments in the Church of England over recent years has been the widespread emergence of a new layer of leadership and ministry, variously termed the leadership team, pastoral team, ministry team or eldership.

This development is perhaps the most concrete expression of a more widely articulated desire to move away from an expectation that ministry will emanate primarily from a lone clergyperson towards a more collaborative understanding of ministry. Its most prominent—and most prolific—exponent has been Robin Greenwood in his *Transforming Priesthood, Practising Community* (in my view the clearest presentation of his thought), *The Ministry Team Handbook* and *Transforming Church*.[1]

Greenwood provides both a helpful generic umbrella term 'Ministry Leadership Teams' (MLTs) and a concise definition:

> Ministry Leadership Teams consist of those in ordained and licensed ministry and others who, together and in diversity, lead, encourage and build up the work of the whole Body of Christ.[2]

MLTs are distinct from Team ministries, which consist primarily of groups of clergy serving a number of congregations. They also differ significantly from Staff Teams, which consist mainly of full and part-time workers serving a large congregation. MLTs emerged initially in several local congregations in the late 60s and 70s.[3] However, in recent years, several of the dioceses which have developed schemes for ordained local ministry (OLM) have decided that this is only to be permitted in parishes which have first developed an MLT. They have therefore invested significantly in promoting and supporting such teams. Some of these dioceses also encourage MLTs which meet certain criteria to be formally mandated by the bishop. This is intended to make any future incumbents see such teams as part of a settled, externally authorized pattern of ministry, rather than (as happened often in the earlier experiments) something that can be easily folded should it prove in any way uncongenial.

Those who have heard a presentation by a diocesan local ministry officer, or read any of the published writing (most of which is produced by those holding such roles) will have heard many benefits of teams being trumpeted.

Pastoral Visiting

An increase in pastoral visiting is often one of the first concrete achievements of teams. There may be an initial hesitancy from parishioners at receiving visits by someone other than the vicar, but in time most come to appreciate the increased coverage that can be given once a greater number of people have been trained, mobilized and co-ordinated. This area of ministry is also one that a large proportion of team members often feel comfortable with, as it represents a natural extension of the good neighbourliness and Christian caring that they have probably been undertaking for many years previously.

Mission Projects

There are countless mission initiatives that are reported as having been initiated by Leadership teams too, including:

- youth clubs;
- *Alpha* courses;
- schemes for baptism or marriage preparation and follow up;
- additional services (perhaps reflecting a different style of worship from that previously offered).

Prayer

When an MLT is formed, team members often feel a greater sense of responsibility for the well-being of their church, and team meetings can form a natural place to pray together. In parishes where there have not previously been small groups meeting for study, prayer or fellowship, these aspects of team meetings may well be a real source of spiritual growth and excitement.

Individual Ministries

Many MLT members will speak of the way in which being chosen by the congregation and authorized by the bishop has increased their confidence to be involved in service and ministry. In addition, part of the ethos of most of the current diocesan schemes is to encourage MLT members to consider becoming trained and authorized as local ministers. In Lichfield diocese, for example, as a well as the traditional role of reader, individuals can also become OLMs, outreach leaders, pastoral care leaders, prayer guides and adult educators/trainers.

Clergy Support and Hope

The literature reports many teams which have given previously over-stretched clergy new support and hope. *Dynamic Local Ministry* describes one incumbent, 'Stephen' who struggled with organizing church life and making the most of the gifts of others. He was attracted to the idea of an MLT, however, and found:

> The best thing for Stephen was that, at the Team's first meeting, he suddenly realized that for the first time in years he was not expected to take the chair, provide input, take notes or act as secretary. He just had to be prayerful and wise![4]

Diocesan Support

The early experiments in MLTs were in single parishes, where the team generally had little recognition or backup from the wider church. By contrast the recent initiatives at diocesan level provide external consultancy, training, authorization and support. The benefits listed above, as well as being widely broadcast to encourage more parishes to come on board, are also being used in some quarters to proclaim that a way forward is being found for development of Anglican ministry both in these particular dioceses and (by implication) nationally.

Personally I do not doubt the reality of some of these benefits. However, my own observations yield a far less rosy picture than that described in the literature and presentations. There are a number of teams which have been a significant source of conflict in their parishes. Many 'medium performing' teams do not yet seem to have repaid the time and energy invested in them. Far from providing a release from previous burdens on clergy, managing and leading the team in many instances seems simply to add to the long list of tasks to be done. Even in the more obviously 'successful' teams, significant tensions and differences of understanding can sometimes be observed.

Specific problems seem to recur in a number of areas and these are explored further in the supporting material at www.grovebooks.co.uk. There is not space here to deal with the complex issue of selection of team members. Despite many dioceses devising complex selection procedures to ensure that all are consulted,[5] these have not always produced an effective team. In this booklet I focus on the following areas of concern:

- expectations and roles;
- relationship to incumbent (which often causes particular problems when a new appointment is made) and to the PCC;
- renewal of team membership.

2

There are Teams...and Teams: A Classification of MLTs

There is a huge variety of different types of teams in operation.

This is seen by several writers and advisors as highly beneficial—a far more truly *local* approach than would be the case if there were a single approved model of operation. The following analysis of MLTs identifies three key areas of difference.

Motivation

Tiller cited three main factors which have drawn attention to the possibilities of shared leadership in local churches:[6]

- The need to build up a truly indigenous church in urban priority areas.
- The disappearance of the resident parson from many villages.
- The need to provide adequate pastoral care where there is a large population and a growing church.

Tiller's contention was that 'between them these three factors are relevant to the majority of parishes in the Church of England.' However, this blurs the fact that there is highly unlikely to be more than one of these factors in operation in any context, and that each of these represents a significantly different motivation.

- In addition, many MLTs have been set up in parishes where none of these factors is present—small to medium-sized churches in socially mixed or decidedly middle class areas—which still have a full-time incumbent. Here it is clearly still possible to operate some kind of single-handed ministry, and so the primary motivation must be theological or ideological rather than pragmatic.
- In some dioceses, as the institution of a formal leadership team is a pre-requisite to the appointment of an ordained local minister (OLM), many teams have been primarily driven by this factor.

A further distinction, that may be particularly important in the early stages of team development, is whether the setting up of the team was mainly driven by the incumbent or others.

Role

This is perhaps the most important distinction between different teams and the cause of most confusion too. A survey of the literature, combined with my own observations, suggests that the roles adopted by MLTs can be divided into the following main areas of activity.

a) Pastoral

This is most likely to involve visiting church contacts who are known to have particular needs: the bereaved, sick or housebound. However, more ambitious attempts at pastoral care may include visits to church contacts, electoral roll members, or even in some cases to all who live in the parish. Where pastoral care is one of the MLT's primary roles, the team could provide an important possible forum both for initial training and for ongoing support and supervision.

b) Mission Oriented

Here MLTs seek to initiate and run significant new projects, such as clubs for the elderly or young people; a regular all age service; organizing preparation and follow up for baptism or marriage contacts.

c) Heads of Department

This term is often used to describe an MLT where the team is comprised of people who hold a responsibility for a section of the church's life.

i) This may mean that team members are office holders in preexisting church roles—churchwardens, Readers, Sunday club co-ordinator, home group co-ordinator, Boys' Brigade company leader.

ii) In other cases, after appointment to the team, each member is given a broad area of church life to 'supervise,' such as worship, teaching, outreach, social concern, or pastoral care.

d) Think Tank

This description implies that team membership is primarily about generating new ideas, and does not necessarily involve a commitment to ongoing involvement in new projects. This may well be a more realistic self-understanding where the team consists of people with existing heavy commitments. It is worth noting, however, that Greenwood's writing questions the validity of a team that is no more than a think tank; for him an MLT should function as a 'ministering body' rather than merely in the realm of ideas.[7]

e) Liturgical

This is the most common primary emphasis in multi-benefice contexts, where a team's main goal is to maintain, or even increase, the core activity of leading and preaching at worship.

In some cases team meetings may be taken up by detailed planning for specific services. More commonly, an MLT whose main focus is on worship will use team meetings to agree rotas, or to discuss broader matters of mutual concern—such as the introduction of new music or liturgy, or to attempt to give feedback on one another's sermons.

Each of these five areas is important and the injection of an enthusiastic team of people to tackle them offers huge potential for growth. However, unless a high proportion of the team's members have a great deal of spare time and energy, it is unlikely that a team will be able to work effectively in more than 2 (or at most 3) of these areas. It is therefore important that those promoting teams do not paint an unrealistic picture of what might be achievable. Greenwood seems to me to be particularly guilty of this in his case studies, in which the volume and variety of tasks achieved bear little relation to what I have seen.[8]

In most real-life church contexts, the setting-up process must therefore prioritize which roles it would like the MLT to tackle—bearing in mind who might be available to serve on it. Ideally this would take place before the final selection of team members, as this can then enable those with the appropriate gifts to be chosen. For some of the roles, a mixture of gifts will of course be necessary, and the question of membership and roles is explored further in the online resources at www.grovebooks.co.uk.

Further Questions Raised by Each Possible Team Role

Each of these areas of work and ministry raises significantly different questions, many of which would be helpfully addressed at early stage in the team's inception.

a) Pastoral

In some contexts, those visited may take some time to accept the validity of pastoral care from a lay person. Team members may well need a degree of resilience to cope with this. Occasionally clergy can unconsciously encourage these attitudes.

In dioceses where the term 'Leadership teams' has become the norm, it is also questionable whether a team whose primary role is in pastoral care sits comfortably with this title.

b) Mission Oriented
In most churches a group of people offering to initiate and staff new projects is unlikely to be controversial. Presumably the norm will be to seek the PCC's approval before going ahead with anything new. If the projects are mostly short-term, then such a group may continue in this role indefinitely. However if longer-term projects are in mind, it may also be wise to consider what may happen after the first two or three significant new long-term projects are initiated. One option might be for each of these projects to have their own management teams—maybe even for the MLT to disband. Alternatively this group could then evolve into operating primarily as a 'heads of department' meeting.

c) Heads of Department
Though the title 'heads of department' is helpful in clarifying that team membership is related to particular roles in the life of the church, it actually says very little about the purpose of the team itself.

- In some cases the purpose of team meetings may be no more than encouragement, sharing and prayer among team members, who each retain full autonomy over their particular departments. In such situations, even though the team may have few concrete achievements to boast about, it may actually provide a very constructive support for leaders who had previously felt overburdened or isolated.

- At the other extreme, a 'heads of department' meeting could represent a form of managerial control with the main purpose of meetings being for the incumbent, or other leader, to impart instructions to team members, with little scope for real discussion or dissent.

- Alternatively the group may develop a significant leadership role in itself—either of the overall life of the church or in determining the policy which the individual heads of department are to follow. However, for any team members in roles which had previously been autonomous, or solely accountable to the incumbent, becoming accountable to a group in this way may represent a significant adjustment.

d) Think Tank

A MLT which includes this role will need to define its relationship with the PCC particularly carefully. This issue is discussed in more detail in chapter 4.

e) Liturgical

Problems and tensions are most likely to occur if:

i) The agenda behind the setting up of the team is to significantly alter the style of worship of existing services

ii) Team members are slow to develop competence in leading worship

iii) Decisions about worship were previously made more broadly, for example by the PCC.

Relationship to Incumbent

Those promoting leadership teams have a wide variety of underlying understandings about the role of the incumbent. For some, there is a presumption that he or she will continue to exercise a significant individual leadership role both in the local church and in the MLT. This undoubtedly remains the formal legal position.

However, for many of those promoting teams, the whole *raison d'être* of MLTs is undermined by this notion. For them, if a team is to be truly collaborative, the incumbent must stop trying to be a leader, and seek to evolve into a facilitator to enable a truly *local* leadership to have the dominant role in the church's life. Many envisage the eventual goal of this process being for the incumbent to virtually work him or herself out of a job—either because their traditional role is seen as ideologically undesirable or, as Tiller suggested, no longer affordable, or lacking the manpower required.[9]

A mismatch in assumptions in a local church can cause huge problems

These differing understandings about the relationship between the MLT and the incumbent are present too at a local level among both incumbents and among other MLT members. Where there is a mismatch of assumptions in a local church this can cause huge problems; this appears to be one of the main reasons why so many teams struggle to adjust to the arrival of a new incumbent.

Digging Deeper: The Underlying Ideology and Theology of MLTs 3

Pragmatic Reasons for the Development of MLTs

One reason for the encouragement of MLTs in many dioceses is undoubtedly pragmatic; it is hard to see how else to respond responsibly to the current state of the local church life. Though there are some churches which are shining exceptions, the fact is that many congregations are declining at the kind of rate that, if continued, will make it impossible for them to support a full-time stipendiary incumbent on a reasonable wage in the next generation. Inherited assets can provide only limited subsidies and larger churches are rightly seeing the need to limit the amount of cross-subsidy that they can responsibly offer without inhibiting their own effectiveness.

The development of local ministry can be seen as a responsible preparation for the future

In the short term, the sharing of professional ministry between two or more congregations is of course the most obvious option and this is already well underway, especially in rural areas. However, if the underlying understanding of ministry as emanating primarily from a paid individual is not altered, then the recent history of the Methodist and URC churches would seem to confirm that decline may well accelerate as each parish is able to call on less and less professional time.[10]

For many smaller churches therefore, the local ministry movement seems to provide the only viable alternative. In some cases it might be hoped that the sharing of ministry and leadership would result in the re-invigoration of church life and finances. However, even where numerical decline, sadly, continues, the development of local ministry can be seen as a responsible preparation for the future. In these cases it will represent an attempt to re-invent the local church as a organization that is primarily run by volunteers, and so can continue unburdened with the need to provide a professional stipend. This is of course a very difficult transition but there is nothing inherent to the Christian faith about leaders being paid and it is surely right for the church at a diocesan and national level to at least allow local churches to attempt to remodel themselves in this way.

Despite this undoubtedly pragmatic imperative, most of the literature also attempts some kind of justification of the development of MLTs on biblical and theological grounds.

Greenwood's Trinitarian Approach

The most heavyweight and influential recent writing which touches significantly on this question is Greenwood's *Transforming Priesthood*. This puts forward a trinitarian basis for the church's future direction:

> An ecclesiology for a church which is a sign and a foretaste of God's final ordering of all things in Christ will be informed and nurtured by a social trinitarianism.[11]

This leads to many conclusions with which the present writer would agree wholeheartedly. Greenwood is surely right in his critique of the type of Anglicanism that sees church membership solely as a private means to securing God's blessing. He helpfully points out that, by contrast, the Scriptures reveal a key part of the divine plan to be the creation of a church community, as a reflection of the supremely relational nature of the trinity. Furthermore, Greenwood offers a robust refutation of models of ministry that dominated the Church of England during the twentieth century which believed that the priest had an ontological priority over the laity.

However, there are problems with Greenwood's approach. If a truly biblical trintarianism were applied to the relationship between clergy and laity, then the willing obedience of the son displayed in the garden of Gesthemene narrative[12] or in John 6.38[13] could in fact offer considerable support to the 'father knows best' style of ministry. Furthermore, Greenwood's style of argumentation from the nature of the trinity into a supposedly 'trinitarian ecclesiology' seems to be so imprecise as to permit almost any conclusions to be reached. And one is left with the suspicion that Greenwood's trinitarian ecclesiology in fact represents no more than an impressive theological veneer to buttress convictions about collaborative ministry which are, in fact, held on rather different grounds.

Biblical Patterns of Ministry

Other attempts at a theological undergirding of MLTs draw helpfully on the many strands of New Testament thought that emphasize the principle that ministry belongs to the whole body of Christ. 1 Corinthians 12 and Romans 12.3–8 are particularly significant in correcting an understanding of Christian ministry which was almost exclusively focussed on the work of the ordained.

However, though these texts are foundational in providing a basis for shared ministry generally, they do not in themselves provide the basis for forming a team—which by definition includes only some members of the congregation. They do not really touch on the question of leadership either. If anything, the body metaphor, as it is expressed in 1 Corinthians 12 and Romans 12, would suggest a single individual taking much of the decision-making and co-ordination role, much as a single organ, the brain, does in the human body. The quest for a biblical undergirding of the *leadership* role of MLTs therefore requires a rather broader exploration of models of leadership in Scripture.

Old Testament Leadership and the Elders

One line of enquiry sometimes used to justify the contemporary developments of MLTs is to point to the pervasive OT references to elders.[14] This seems initially to offer support for what is happening today, as even when the term 'eldership' is deliberately avoided, there are strong parallels between MLT members and elders in the OT—both being a plural, grass root leadership institution. Furthermore, influential OT theologians including Martin Noth[15] have championed the eldership, proposing an even more significant historical role than the text itself suggests.

More often than not in the Old Testament, God leads through a single individual

However, an approach which accepts the Old Testament canon as Scripture must surely record that God's leadership of his people in the Old Testament, more often than not, is presented as being mediated through a single individual. If there were no collective models of leadership, this might not be seen as significant—there was no group for God to work through. But the fact that God works through individuals—despite the existence of the eldership—on reflection would lend more support to individual models of leadership than to collective patterns.

Leadership in the New Testament

In the New Testament, the situation is more complex. In previous centuries each denomination was inclined to see its own structure of ecclesiastical government as explicitly legitimated in Scripture. However, more recently the prevailing critical orthodoxy has taken an exactly opposite approach—to see merely a confused multiplicity of models emerging in different parts of the New Testament. This often leads to the conclusion that each church is free to make its own judgment on pragmatic grounds about what models of leadership will best resonate with the prevailing culture.[16]

The Pauline Material

Most 20th century Protestant scholarship saw the uncontested Pauline epistles as reflecting and authenticating a purely charismatic form of church organization in which the possession of appropriate spiritual gifts was the sole criterion for the exercise of leadership.[17] On this understanding the Pastoral Epistles, the Gospel of Luke, and other later biblical material which envisage the formal appointment of leaders, are seen to represent a regrettable departure from Paul's charismatic ideal.

However, though the charismatic principle is undoubtedly dominant in the uncontested Pauline epistles, nonetheless there are still strong hints that some degree of fixity about leadership was envisaged.[18] Furthermore, this approach effectively denies any real authority to the Pastoral Epistles—which are, after all, still recognized throughout the Christian church as part of the New Testament canon. Indeed it could well be argued that these should be given greater weight than the earlier material, because they represent a more mature reflection on how churches can balance the tension between the ministry of the whole body and the need to prevent anarchy. Furthermore, they also represent a necessary development of local church leadership as the apostles' potential for direct influence in local congregations is diminishing.

This role of the apostles, which is often omitted from discussions of Pauline leadership patterns, is also a hugely important component. In the Corinthian correspondence, Paul does not view the church as an egalitarian utopia. On the contrary, the most obvious reason why he does not appeal to the role of local leaders is because he is still trying to exercise a direct control over the life of the church.

It is of course beyond the scope of this booklet to attempt an exact reconstruction of the patterns of leadership that are reflected in the different New Testament documents. Nonetheless, once this apostolic component is properly acknowledged, it becomes possible to identify a definite consistency in regard to the relationship between individual and corporate leadership over local churches. For in almost all of the NT documents both are present, in creative tension.

The Gospels and Acts

The gospels provide an important confirmation of this thesis, as Jesus' preparation for the church's ministry after his ascension is portrayed in all four gospels as envisaging both a corporate role for the twelve (Mark 3.14–19, Matthew 28.16–20), and a distinctive individual leadership role for Peter (for example Matthew 16.13–19 and John 21.15ff).

The early chapters of Acts show this working in practice. In the later chapters, a similar balance is shown in the description of the Gentile mission. Though Acts is clear that this quickly came to be dominated by the individual leadership of Paul, it was nonetheless not a lone leadership, as it was exercised in conjunction with Barnabas, Silas and others.

In the Acts' account of the council of Jerusalem, the church's decision-making process again exhibits both a corporate and an individual dimension. Here the apostles and elders meet together to consider the vexed question of admission of the Gentiles, but what might otherwise have been an impossible impasse was resolved by the individual leadership of James, whose judgement is seen as binding.

Acts exhibits both a corporate and an individual dimension to decision-making

The Pastoral Epistles

The leadership models being advocated by the Pastoral Epistles are hotly debated. Campbell contends that a central purpose of the letters is to establish the legitimacy of a single bishop in each local church, acting over and above a team of elders, and as a replacement for apostolic oversight.[19] However, the dominant view is still that the terms *'episkopos'*(bishop) and *'presbuteros'*(elder) should be viewed as synonymous, with the author of the Pastorals being seen as proposing that local churches should be led by a group of peers. What is often forgotten though is that, even if Campbell's thesis is rejected, there is still an individual leadership envisaged in the life of these congregations—namely that of the purported recipients of the letters, Timothy and Titus. For these individuals' supervisory roles, though never explicitly articulated, are constantly implied.[20]

Early Church History

One objection to the recent developments in collaborative ministry comes from those of a more catholic persuasion who see such changes as threatening the central role of the three-fold order of bishops, priests and deacons. But it is worth remembering that this three-fold order originally existed in a single town or city. So even where the bishop was held to have a very dominant role, the original operation of the three-fold order did in fact contain some collaborative elements.[21] Indeed Croft takes this line of thought one step further in arguing that recent developments should be seen to represent a return to the kind of collegiality that the three-fold order originally enshrined.[22]

Contemporary Leadership Theory and Models

The need for individual leadership, even in enterprises and teams that are intrinsically corporate, is also reflected in much secular thinking. This is shown in the considerable volume of recent writing on how to be an effective individual leader, leading John Adair to conclude:

> It is now widely accepted that the most important role in a small work group is that of a leader…The role is to help the group achieve its common task, to maintain it as a unity and to ensure that each individual contributes his best.[23]

In practice too, a very wide variety of contemporary organizations display this balance between individual and collective leadership. In the political sphere, though systems of democracy differ, they all include an identifiable individual leader. The standard model for managing a company similarly involves decisions being taken not by a board of directors acting as equals, but led by a chairperson and/or managing director. In the sphere of public service, especially in education, the potential for a single individual leader to effect change is widely acknowledged.

Conclusion

The current movement towards a more collegial style of leadership than that which has prevailed for most of the church's history is entirely justified. However, both the New Testament and current secular thought point strongly towards the continuing need for individual leadership, even when operating collaborative patterns of work and ministry. Churches should think very carefully before taking on board—either consciously or subconsciously—an egalitarianism which denigrates the role of individual leadership.

What kind of collegiality? What kind of balance between individual and collective leadership? How large should the collegial body be, and how should it be chosen? These are of course very important questions, and different strands of biblical material, and different periods in the life of the early church, represent very different answers to these questions. We need to admit that we have most decidedly not found a blueprint for church order. Nonetheless in demonstrating, from the New Testament material at least, a common thread of the importance for local churches in having both individual and collegial dimensions to leadership we have, I believe, defined some helpful parameters.

Further exploration of biblical patterns and their relation to contemporary practice can be found in the online resources at www.grovebooks.co.uk.

Practicalities 4

Where Does the Vicar Fit In?

A Sharing of Ministry

For some churches and incumbents (or equivalent), even the notion of shared ministry will require a significant re-orientation. This need will be greatest where previously only the ordained have been understood as undertaking Christian ministry; the roles of others being seen as intrinsically secondary in practical or support tasks. In many other contexts, though the language of ministry may be used more broadly, there can still be an underlying assumption among either clergy or laity that the ministry of the ordained is intrinsically superior. Though such an attitude can co-exist with an MLT, in time it will need to be altered, both for the ministry of team members (and others) to be able to reach their full potential, and also to release the ordained from the burden of unrealistic expectations.

A one-man bottleneck can simply be replaced with a five-person bottleneck

One danger that needs to be particularly watched is if the broadening of ministry is seen to extend only as far as members of the MLT, or worse only to OLMs. This would seem to be a particular danger of using the term 'ministry team,' but may well apply in other contexts too. As Philip King helpfully points out, a one-man bottleneck can simply be replaced by a five-person bottleneck, with other church members having to wait up to 3 or 4 weeks until the next team meeting before their concerns can even begin to be addressed.[24]

A Sharing of Control

I have argued not for a complete transfer of power away from the incumbent but rather for a balance between the individual leadership and direction of an incumbent and the collegial leadership of others. However, at different points of the New Testament this balance appears to lie in different places— on some occasions more with the collective group and on others more with an individual. It seems wise, therefore, to see room for a considerable diversity to pertain in different local contexts today, providing that some kind of balance is maintained.

This represents a significantly different understanding from some of the contemporary literature, which sees a balance of power between individual and collective leadership as legitimate only as part of a journey towards a completely egalitarian ideal. This may be diagrammatically represented as follows:

Domination by Incumbent	Steps along the way towards collaborative ministry → → → Desirable direction of movement							Genuinely collaborative leadership. (*ie* Incumbent functioning solely in enabling role)
1	2	3	4	5	6	7	8	9	10

By comparison, this booklet is arguing for the same data to be interpreted in a rather different way:

Domination by Incumbent	Legitimate area of diversity in collaborative ministry ← either direction of → movement considered acceptable and desirable depending on needs of congregation							Incumbent either not allowed, or chooses not to exercise any significant leadership
1	2	3	4	5	6	7	8	9	10

A Sharing of Leadership Roles
So far, the sharing of leadership has been discussed mainly in terms of decision making power. Robert Daborn has recently put forward a model in which the multiplicity of different leadership roles taken on by an incumbent are identified, with a view to enabling different components to be taken on by different members of a leadership team. These roles are as follows:

- Liturgical leader
- Team chair/leader, aiming to ensure that the team is true to its purpose in terms of task, integration and membership
- Enabling leader, with a central role of discerning and enabling the ministerial gifts of the whole congregation
- Project leader—taking responsibility for a particular piece of work
- Presiding leader—acting as a focal figure whom the congregation naturally regards as its leader[25]

This is a very interesting proposal. However, in many small and medium-sized churches (of under, say, 100 regular worshippers), there may well be a very limited pool from which team members can be drawn. As a result, teams may have to include people at a very early stage in their leadership development or with significant areas of personal insecurity and immaturity or who are inclined to dominate others. In such cases, this sharing of leadership roles may prove rather problematic.

Questions to Consider

1 When new ideas are implemented in your church, what proportion of them originated from (a) the incumbent (b) somebody else?

2 What happens when your incumbent's proposal does not immediately win widespread approval? What proportion of the time does it (a) get forced through anyway (b) eventually get accepted, as others are keen to trust the vicar on at least some things (c) effectively get withdrawn?

3 Is this a healthy situation? If you have an MLT how effective would you judge it to be in complementing the incumbent's leadership?

But What About the PCC?

The development of MLTs does not, of course, represent the first attempt at encouraging shared leadership in local congregations in the recent history of the Church of England. For over 80 years, democratically elected church councils have been a legally binding requirement in each parish. Why then, the need for MLTs?

Where PCCs Have Failed

Church law states 'It shall be the duty of the minister and the PCC to consult together on matters of general concern and importance to the parish.'[26] The PCC's first function is subsequently defined to be: 'co-operation with the minister in promoting in the parish the whole mission of the church, pastoral, evangelistic, social and ecumenical.'

But in practice, the PCC's role in decision-making can still be very limited. In some settings this situation will have been engineered by the incumbent, either with overt threats that any deviation from his or her wishes represents a disloyalty to God or by a more subtle engineering of the PCC agendas. In other settings, an incumbent who is genuinely keen to encourage collaborative decision-making may find that even highly educated PCC members wish to defer to his or her opinion.

Furthermore, even when PCCs have been effective in promoting shared decision-making, they have often not helped congregations to develop other dimensions of shared leadership and ministry. This is partly to do with the large size of most church councils, which render them unsuited to exercising detailed pastoral oversight. In addition, a culture has arisen in many churches which sees election to the PCC more as an expression of democratic rights—providing a check on the executive—than as conferring any responsibility to be actively involved in leadership and ministry.

One possible response to this is to attempt to alter the culture of PCCs and reduce their size, so that they are better able to exercise an active leadership role in collaboration with the incumbent. Another option is to attempt to develop the standing committee's role so that it begins to set a collective lead in the local church. But changing the culture of existing structures can be very hard, and there are certain legal restraints about what would be permitted too. The alternative—setting up MLTs in parallel to PCCs—seems far simpler. It does, however, raise important questions regarding the relationship between the authority of the leadership team and the PCC.[27]

Greenwood's suggestion is that the PCC might develop a 'diaconal' in contrast to an MLT's 'apostolic' role.[28] This would leave PCCs concentrating mainly on practical matters, such as fabric and finance, whilst allowing the MLT to have a free hand in the more central aspects of the church's life such as matters of worship and mission.

In Church law there can at present be no formal transfer of power away from the PCC

In Church law, however, there can at present be no formal transfer of power away from the PCC. Hence, after a limited discussion of the issues raised, the Lichfield diocesan handbook *Implementing the Local Ministry Scheme* draws almost the exactly opposite conclusion to Greenwood, namely that 'The PCC, not the Team, is the decision-making body.'[29] Others churches operating teams have reached a similar position, concluding that the PCC should retain full control over church policy, with the MLT responsible only for its implementation. The problem with these positions, though, is that they seem incompatible with the use of the word 'leadership' in many teams' official title.

Tensions between the PCC and MLT emerged recently as a major issue in the parish where I serve as vicar. Members of the PCC who were not members of the team expressed resentment if they felt that they were not being allowed an equal say in the decision-making process. However, at the same time, members of the leadership team became frustrated if other PCC members wanted to re-open discussions that had already taken place in the MLT. Biblical teaching within the church on the servant nature of leadership may soften some of these conflicts between different church bodies—but they are still there nonetheless.

It is also important to note that, ironically, the potential for conflict between the authority of a PCC and leadership team may well be greatest for churches in which the PCC has come furthest along the road of exercising a genuinely collaborative leadership role. In this case, the transfer of some of the PCC's power to a smaller group, whose make-up may well not be so clearly democratic, may rightly be questioned. It could be that such a PCC concludes that, though they are committed to the same kind of ideals and goals, they do not need an MLT as they are already providing an effective expression of collaborative ministry and leadership. This could well be the wisest course too in churches where the standing committee has developed a significant leadership role.

If, however, a PCC does decide to set up a leadership team it should surely face up to the fact that, if the group it is to fulfil the role that its name implies, there must be some practical diminution of the PCC's say in some areas. The church council may formally retain the final say in decision-making and always have the right to veto a leadership team's proposal or to re-examine their thinking. However, this right will need to be used selectively, and the PCC members need to be willing, more often than not, to trust the leadership team's conclusions.

Questions to Consider

1   If your church has an MLT, what proportion of MLT ideas are:
    (a) implemented without even being put before the PCC?
    (b) accepted by the PCC without much discussion or 'on trust'?
    (c) scrutinized in detail by the PCC?
    (d) rejected by the PCC?

2   What would you consider to be a healthy balance of answers to question 1?

How Long, O Lord?

There are two strongly conflicting principles at work here, which have not yet been satisfactorily confronted or resolved. The first is the tradition that Christian ministry is a lifelong vocation. This is at its most acute among those with a 'catholic' doctrine of priesthood, in which ordination is seen to effect an indelible ontological change on an individual. But a similar deep conviction is also prevalent more subtly—even among those of a very 'low' church tradition who would eschew such theological ideas. I used to visit an elderly Methodist lady who had not been involved in active public ministry for over 10 years, and yet introduced herself by saying 'I am *(note tense)* a lay preacher you know.'

The introduction of licences and formal review processes for readers and clergy has not significantly changed this core conviction. Even if a clergyperson is unable to secure an incumbency, he or she will invariably be given continuing 'permission to officiate.' A reader's position may seem more vulnerable but PCCs and incumbents are very reluctant to terminate a reader's contract and may well approve of a fresh agreement at the quinquennial review, even where they have serious reservations about the value of the individual's ministry. This is part of what Handy calls the 'person' culture of the church.[30]

There appears to be a desire for the newer forms of local authorized ministry to be seen in a similar light—as a lifelong divine calling which is recognized by the congregation, rather than as a time-limited appointment to a particular office or role. In the case of OLMs this is because a large majority of the Church of England would find it very hard to accept a limited-contract priest as in any sense a 'proper' priest. In the case of dioceses experimenting with newer forms of authorized lay ministry,[31] it almost certainly stems from the desire for these ministries to be put on an equal footing with Readership.

However, there is a conflicting current of thought present too, representing a more managerial or functional approach to ministry. Here, the damage done by those who remain in office long after they have ceased to function effectively (typically as incumbents or churchwardens) has led to moves to discourage such appointments from being seen as for life. This thinking has been enshrined in the Churchwarden's Measure 2001, which states that after 6 successive years in office, a person is ordinarily ineligible to stand for re-election for the next two years.

In the case of OLMs the attempt is sometimes made to resolve the conflict between these two competing ideologies by distinguishing between the lifelong character of the vocation and the temporary nature of the licence. However, it is doubtful whether this distinction is really tenable; it seems unlikely to provide much consolation to an OLM refused a licence to continue in active ministry, and hence it is surely unlikely that licences will ever be terminated, except in the most extreme of circumstances.

Stranger in the Wings, a central review of OLM ministry, acknowledges the concern that an OLM is effectively granted a lifelong position in a congregation, and so could become a stagnating influence in their parish, thwarting any visionary or prophetic plans of an incoming stipendiary.[32] This situation could easily arise too in an MLT without OLMs if membership came, in practice, to be seen as being for life.

Stranger in the Wings' response is that this problem can be averted by continuing ministerial training and by regular monitoring and review. However, as we have seen, such processes can quickly become a formality. It may require considerable skill and subtlety on the part of the reviewer to encourage a person who probably ought to take a step back from active leadership to reflect objectively on their ministry without creating a great deal of ill-feeling. One very experienced incumbent I spoke to had achieved this by increasing the regularity of reviews with some individuals to as often as every six months, repeatedly asking how they felt about the relevant area of ministry, until eventually they drew their own conclusions. This method needs the incumbent to exercise considerable sensitivity and patience; even then it may well only work when the incumbent is loved and trusted in the first place.

Perhaps the only tenable alternative is to create a category of ministry parallel to that of the 'reader emeritus'

In the case of team members who are OLMs, it may be questionable whether even the most persistent review process can really counter the power of the prevailing perception that priesthood is for life. Perhaps the only tenable alternative is to create a category of ministry parallel to that of the 'reader emeritus,' or of the retired stipendiary who is given permission to officiate. This would allow an individual to be engaged in most of the individual ministerial tasks of an OLM, whilst also gently implying that they may not expect to have such a prominent role in the leadership of a congregation.

For non-ordained MLT members there is the opportunity to create a culture, both in the local church, and in the diocese, in which their appointment is not seen as being lifelong, either in theory or in practice. This will of course create an undesirable inequality between lay and ordained local ministers, but it is hard to see any other way of avoiding the strong possibility of many leadership teams in the future inhibiting, rather than enabling, the development of a local church's life and mission. Dioceses will have a key role to play in facilitating this culture by providing recommended mechanisms for regular re-evaluation of team membership which do not presume that re-appointment will be the norm.

Learning from the Nonconformist Experience

My own experience growing up in the United Reformed Church (URC) suggests that avoiding stagnation and creating a healthy turn-around of leaders is not a minor concern. I understand too that this issue has led many Baptist churches to move away from the perception that membership of the diaconate should be for life towards seeing one or two five-year terms as the norm.

However, I found almost no recognition in any of the Anglican literature about the need to learn from the non-conformist experience. Even in the more analytical and reflective material, there is hardly any acknowledgement that the sharing of leadership represents a path that has been travelled before.

The sharing of leadership represents a path that has been travelled down before

This may be partly explained by the fear that the comparison could be politically unwise, giving further ammunition to those who see the development of MLTs as un-Anglican. It may also be explained by the fact that the denomination which has practised shared leadership for longest, and which in other respects (such as its broad mixture of church tradition) is most like Anglicanism is the URC. This denomination has sadly been declining even faster than the C of E over the last 50 years. At the very least this calls into question the simplistic conviction that all of the C of E's problems can be reversed by a move towards a more collaborative leadership. More radically, it might also be worth investigating if there are ways in which the URC's emphasis on collective leadership could even have contributed to its recent decline.

Questions to Consider

1 Who would you like to see involved in your church's leadership in 20 years' time? How can you make this happen?

2 How can a person tell when it might be right to step down to make way for others? Why do some people find this hard to do? What can be done to help?

Where Do We Go From Here? 5

Recommendations to Dioceses Promoting MLTs

It is important for dioceses that are investing significant resources into promoting and supporting MLTs at some point to pause and honestly review their effectiveness. For such reviews to be objective they will need to avoid being dominated by those involved in promoting local ministry.

Part of the review process would be to evaluate the ideology and assumptions being passed on by the training. As I have already intimated, my own view is that the denigration of the incumbent's role as individual leader, and the promotion of an egalitarian ideal—which is at odds with the continuing legal position in the Church of England—is responsible for a number of the problems in implementation in parishes. At the very least, even if some steer is given towards a particular viewpoint, the variety of understandings about the relationship between individual and corporate leadership should be neutrally expressed. This would have the merits of enabling those being trained for local ministry to cope better with the actual views of their incumbents.

Part of the review process would be to evaluate the ideology and assumptions being passed on by the training

Dioceses which have encouraged a wide variety of types of leadership teams might also do well to reflect further on the implications of this diversity. Though there are many advantages to this approach, it is likely to cause problems when incumbents used to one model of team operation move to work in a parish where a team has been set up on a very different basis. It may help simply for a team's actual functioning role and relationships to be better documented in the parish profile—perhaps using the analysis from chapter 2 above. But this may not provide all the answers, and there are inherent problems in fostering a fully 'local' approach to ministry in a denomination which has a diocesan and a national dimension to it as well.

Perhaps the most important issue that needs to be examined is whether leadership teams really help churches to be more outward looking and so more effective in their mission to further God's kingdom. The research I have been able to undertake for this booklet has not been comprehensive enough to put forward a definite view on this crucial question. Nonetheless, I have to say that the signs are not as encouraging as I would have hoped them to be.

Are medium-performing MLTs really assisting this transition to a more outwardly-oriented church?

Inevitably leadership teams that are obviously struggling consume far more clergy and lay time and energy than they ever repay. By contrast, high-performing MLTs set up in parishes where there have been 2 or 3 particularly gifted and committed leaders willing to join the team provide an equally obvious net gain. What is less clear is whether the 'medium performing' teams that seem to be more typical are really assisting this transition to a more outwardly-oriented church. The rhetoric used may be that of parish clergy and area advisors 'nurturing and developing lay leadership to enable the ministry of the whole people of God.' The danger is that in practice this could mean concentrating ever more stipendiary resources on the most committed church members, whilst never really releasing enough energy for the work of the kingdom to justify it. If, after allowing several years for MLTs to 'bed in,' this is found to be the reality in the majority of contexts, then MLTs must be judged to have failed and alternative strategies sought.

Even if such drastic action were considered necessary, this would and should not represent the end of the development of every-member ministry. First, this New Testament principle, now that it has been rediscovered, appears theologically incontrovertible. Secondly, some kind of lessening of previous generation's reliance on paid ministry seems essential to the future financial viability of so many small and small-to-medium sized local churches.

What is far more debatable is the demand to move away from any sense of individual leadership (combined with a hostility towards leadership by outsiders) that seems to lie at the root of many understandings of MLTs. Once these demands are questioned, it will be apparent that there are other possible directions for the development of every-member ministry that may be considered:

- Large churches developing paid staff teams already experience a tension between the authority of the staff meeting and that of the PCC. The introduction of an additional authority, namely an MLT of unpaid local leaders may well be viewed in retrospect as adding a burdensome extra management tier, and it may be felt best to concentrate instead on the development of the staff team and PCC.

- By contrast, smaller churches may feel that the tensions between a paid incumbent and the local unpaid leadership are best resolved by dispensing with the role of incumbent altogether. In its place, the church might be led by a team or by an individual—whatever was considered most appropriate—in consultation with the bishop and diocese. (For a full sacramental ministry to be available, this would of course require either permission being granted for lay presidency, or more probably, some continuation of office of OLM.) The main benefit of this pattern would be to enable smaller churches to face the future without the increasingly difficult burden of providing a professional stipend. They might feel able to afford and to benefit from the occasional services of a diocesan or area advisor but unlike an incumbent, their presence would be sufficiently sporadic to avoid any danger of detracting from the authority and ministry of the local church members.

- Medium sized churches may simply decide to be less apologetic about their incumbent exercising, if not sole leadership, then at least a broad measure of individual leadership, provided that it included a commitment to encourage the ministry of others, and some measure of consultation with others through the PCC.

Recommendations to Local Churches

If your church has an MLT exhibiting symptoms of ill-health, it might be worth checking out whether these could be caused by an underlying uncertainty over any of the fundamentals discussed in this booklet, especially regarding:

a) expectations of the team's role(s);
b) the relationship between the incumbent's and the team's authority;
c) the relationship between the PCC and MLT.

If you are thinking of starting up a team, hopefully you will now be rather more aware of some of the pitfalls to avoid. You are unlikely to be able to sort out everything in black and white before you begin (and indeed this could stifle the team's subsequent development). But some careful laying of the foundations, though time-consuming, may help to give your team the best chance of proving itself of value in the long-term.

Notes

1   *Transforming Priesthood* (London: SPCK, 1994); *Practising Community* (London: SPCK, 1996); *The Ministry Team Handbook* (London: SPCK, 2000); *Transforming Church* (London: SPCK, 2002).

2   R Greenwood, *The Ministry Team Handbook* (London: SPCK, 2000) p xi.

3   Some of these early experiments are described in: Cyril Ashton, *Church on the Threshold* (London: Daybreak/DLT, 1991); David Watson, *You are my God* (London: Hodder and Stoughton, 1983) and Michael Saward, *All Change* (London: Hodder and Stoughton, 1983).

4   A Bowden and M West, *Dynamic Local Ministry* (London: Continuum, 2000) p 114.

5   See for example R Greenwood, *The Ministry Team Handbook*, pp 43–44.

6   J Tiller, *A Strategy for the Church's Ministry* (London: CIO publishing, 1983) para 195, pp 116–117.

7   R Greenwood, *The Ministry Team Handbook*, p xvii.

8   R Greenwood ,*The Ministry Team Handbook,* pp xix–xiii. S Croft's opening chapter of *Transforming Communities* (London: DLT, 2002) pp 3–14 is in danger of being similarly unrealistic.

9   See J Tiller, *A Strategy for the Church's Ministry*, especially p 73.

10 See also S Croft, *Transforming Communities*, pp 52–4.

11 R Greenwood, *Transforming Priesthood* (London: SPCK, 1994) p 86.

12 (Luke 22.42) 'Father, if you are willing, take this cup from me; yet not my will, but yours be done.'

13 (John 6.38) 'For I have come down from heaven not to do my will but to do the will of him who sent me.'

14 For example C Skilton, *Leadership Teams* (Grove Pastoral booklet P 78) p 6ff.

15 Summarized in G Bornkamm, 'Presbus' in G Bromiley (ed), *Theological Dictionary of the New Testament Vol VI* (London: Eerdmans, 1964) pp 651–680. See also H Reviv, *The Elders in Ancient Israel* (Jerusalem: Magnes Press, 1989).

16 For example I Bunting, *Models of Ministry* (Grove Pastoral booklet P 54) p 6.

17 The view was first put forward by R Sohm, and more recently articulated by H von Campenhausen and J D G Dunn. For more detail, see R A Campbell, *The Elders: Seniority Within Earliest Christianity* (Edinburgh: T and T Clark, 1994) pp 1–19.

18 For example 1 Thessalonians 5.12. See Campbell, *The Elders* p 97ff.

19 See Campbell, *The Elders* p 176ff.

20 The situation is somewhat more complicated if the letters are deemed to be pseudonymous, and 'Titus' and 'Timothy' to be mere ciphers. But even then the choice of named individuals as ciphers seems to reflect the importance of individual leadership in the author's mind.

21 The subsequent development of the all-powerful lone parish priest is documented in E Schillebeeckx, *The Church with a Human Face: A New and Expanded Theology of Ministry* (London: SCM, 1985) pp 140–1.

22 S Croft, *Ministry in Three Dimensions* (London: Darton Longman and Todd, 1999).

23 J Adair, *Effective Teambuilding* (London: Pan, 1986) p 34.

24 P King, *Leadership Explosion* (London: Hodder and Stoughton, 1987) p 82 and p 105ff.

25 From a sheet entitled 'Collaborative Leadership and Individual Roles' by Robert Daborn, Ministry Advisor in Lichfield Diocese, available online at www.grovebooks.co.uk.

26 The Parochial Church (Powers) Measure 1956, section 2.

27 Despite being raised nearly 20 years ago by Tiller (p 118, para 119), these questions still appear to be a long way from being satisfactorily resolved.

28 Greenwood, *The Ministry Team Handbook,* p 43.

29 p 27.

30 C Handy, *Understanding Voluntary Organizations* (London: Penguin, 1988) p 85ff.

31 See p 4, 'Individual Ministries.'

32 Advisory Board of Ministry, *Stranger in the Wings* (London: Church House Publishing, 1998) p 26.